Ride Out: Crisis Response and Extraction of Human Trafficking Victims
A practical companion guidebook for community leaders and anti-human trafficking organizations (with no need for "Special Ops")

By
RockStarr Ministries

NOTICE: This book is a companion guide for RockStarr Ministries services. It is not meant for amateurs or the merely curious (though they are welcome to read it for information). This book will not make you James Bond or Liam Neeson. This is a book for organizations who are already invested in, and committed to, offering a ride out to victims of human trafficking. Read a lot. Talk to people who are familiar with the issues. Never go into a situation you are only vaguely familiar with.

RSM founder Laurin Crosson was trafficked herself for twenty years and has been running RSM since 2013. She is aware of the dynamics of various situations and risks, and she knows how to communicate with victims, survivors, pimps, and tricks, what to avoid and how to help. Do not attempt to extract victims without the assistance of a Survivor-leader like Laurin who knows the experiences of the clients you provide rides for.

The examples in this book are based on real extractions, though the identifying information has been changed to protect the clientele. Our success rate for extractions is 100% since 2013 when RSM began, with only a tiny minority of recidivism after six months. Since it began, our safe house has had over thirty clients (including the children of more than one mother) stay with us. The vast majority of them have gone on to work or recovery programs, or we have helped them into their own housing situations. Unfortunately we are aware of a few who may have returned to their former life. This deeply saddens us but we are still proud to have shown them that another option exists, and is waiting to help again if and when they become strong enough to make the final move away from that life.

Introduction: The Problem Overall

Human trafficking is a relatively new term in social consciousness, but it is not a new practice. It has gone by other terms, such as "slavery" and "flesh trade." It refers to the control of one person (or many persons) by another, for the economic gain of the "owner" class. It includes the rental of living bodies (the "product" class) for sexual activity, as well as the sale of human beings for the labor or even disposal of the "buyer" class.

Slavery as institution is as old as there are records of human activity, and there has never been a year in which it has not existed. Because it is illegal, real numbers are difficult to collect. Nevertheless, it is generally acknowledged that, like other illegal activities such as illicit drug markets or activities associated with organized crime, human trafficking constitutes a significant portion of economic activity in the world. In the past few years more and more people have become aware that even in the U.S., the sale or rental of human beings is *not* a relic of the pre-Civil War past. While the practice of legally-sanctioned race-based chattel slavery was ended with the Civil War, chattel slavery itself is still thriving in pockets of our country, and is more openly practiced in many areas of the world. The United Nations' modest underestimate is that somewhere between 18 million and 20 million persons around the world were controlled by traffickers, whether for unpaid labor or for sale in the sex trades, or both, from 2010 to 2012 (the last years for which numbers are available ["United Nations Global Report on Trafficking in Persons," New York, 2014]).

With the growing awareness that this heinous practice still exists has come a desire to help change the situation and to help those in the grip of traffickers. But progress has been slow. In 2013, there were over 300,000 beds for stray animals in the United States. There were beds for persons available in over 3,400 domestic violence shelters. However, because "prostitution," the traditional paradigm of most sex-trafficked persons, is still usually seen as a choice and a crime, there were fewer than 400 beds in safe houses for victims of human trafficking. With the awareness of human trafficking on the rise, there is an acute need and desire for more help for victims of traffickers.

But many who want to help these victims are at a loss to know where to begin.

We hope this book will be part of the answer: a short and helpful resource for practical action in the lives of those who would survive human trafficking.

Part 1: It's Not That Complicated

In the past few years, there have been a lot of anti-trafficking organizations who are fairly high-profile featured on the news. These groups are impressive, well-funded, and photogenic. They have engaged widely in large-scale extraction, as well as raising awareness of the problem, and in self-promotion for further actions. Doubtless a number of victims have been helped by them, especially children, and many in far-away countries.

This book has a different focus. The extent to which high-profile groups invest money and resources in special equipment, or in promotional actions, or engaging in military- or SWAT-style "busts," sometimes makes it look like "the" (or the *only*) way to offer help to victims is to have that kind of attention and resources at one's disposal. In this book we want to show that low-key approaches also work, and work steadily, safely. While it's admirable to run a "bust" on an entire brothel or cartel, it can be risky and expensive well beyond what an average community organization can afford, and usually requires police and/or government involvement, planning, and ultimately visibility, which can itself be traumatic for many victims caught in human trafficking.

There is a time and place for SWAT and military-style help, especially in cases involving the State Department, on foreign soil, and in cases of child-trafficking. We applaud these groups who rescue children. But we are also aware of the plights of many victims who are not children. What of them? Does a young victim's birthday suddenly stop the pain she or he feels? Does turning from seventeen to eighteen mean the abuse suffered from the same trick or pimp is now legitimate, or permissible, or painless for the one receiving it? What of victims who are adults, caught for years in trafficker or pimp control, and unwilling or afraid to involve police or high-profile operation tactics?

Many times they live in community with other victims (the phrase is a pimp's "stable" of girls ([and/or boys], as if they were livestock), or they are terrified and unwilling to flip (turn states evidence on) their trafficker. Victims who want to leave the life of cyclical abuse may be afraid of their pimp discovering their plans to leave. They may be afraid of not being able to access services or support outside of the life they've been living. They may be paralyzed by the thought of autonomy, when they have known nothing but external, brutal, control.

Nevertheless, and despite arguments to the contrary from many sources, the majority of trafficked people want to stop being trafficked. They do not have the chance to wait for an army to strategize and execute a tactical invasion of their single dingy motel room. And if they did, it would be a long, long wait. When she is twenty-five, or twenty-nine; when he is thirty-two—when a victim is out of other options and still turning tricks—pushing forty with health problems, wanting and needing to get out—no one comes for them.

We do. You can. This book is our effort to explain a simple and safe approach to extracting victims who seek help to leave, on their own, when no one's army is coming for them. We explain how we have done it: when the survivors we know are ready to leave, we are the ride out. This book describes how to do as we have done—not to try to be vigilantes or "play cops," but how to be a friend to a person who needs a friend; how to respond to a survivor's needs in a low-profile, safe, relatively inexpensive, and effective way to help individual trafficking victims leave their traffickers.

What you won't need:
    *Swat teams.
    *Concealed weapons. (Any weapons)
    *Private investigators.
    *Thousands of dollars.
    *To alert authorities.

*Grandiose, attention-grabbing actions

*Specialized equipment (no cat-burglar stuff, no plastic ties, duct tape, suction-cup glass-climbers, Bowie knives, night-vision goggles, ski masks, HumVees, bull-horns, helicopters, jetskis, tanks, Harrison Ford . . . .)

*Cameras. Especially no cameras! Though cell phone communication can be crucial, in the event of an extraction, it should go without saying that leaving any kind of electronic trail is a bad idea. All participants need to turn off all the social media apps and functions on their phones for safety. The entire effort can be botched by one person neglecting to turn off a device's satellite tracking. Social media alerts of any kind are an absolute nonstarter. This is not about you, ever.

*The attitude that you are a savior. The most important part of this is that you leave behind any ideas you may have about being a "rescuer" or "saving" folks. You may be a brave, generous, noble person with all the good intentions in the world, but if you want to last more than a day at this, let us put this kindly: Get Over Yourself. The rescue is happening in the victim's life, not in your head. However tempting, do not use the language of rescue, when the only job of the extractor is to provide a safe ride out, to a safe place to land. Do not make someone else's situation, life experience, and courage to leave be about you: it is not.

Remember that if you are in a position to help, you already are enjoying freedoms and advantages the trafficking victim does not have. Don't be impressed with yourself for helping. Don't be tempted to add your own ego into the mix. Thinking of yourself as a helper is fine, but thinking of yourself as a rescuer or a savior is offensive. The decisions and actions of a victim in extracting herself or himself is where the focus needs to be. Whether their time in the life was two weeks or ten years, these victims come with needs and trauma that they will have to confront and address for the rest of their lives, many times daily; on a bad day, hourly. If a single rape or trauma requires time and strength to heal, imagine how long years of daily rapes will require. It's not you. They will save themselves. For this you should be grateful; for their efforts you should be in awe.

That said, the single most important element in extraction is the determination of the victim-survivor. They absolutely must be the ones responsible for the rescue and salvation of their own lives. How far they will come and how far they will go is entirely up to them, never you. A survivor can look forward to a lifetime of PTSD-recovery and self-care; investing in themselves and their physical and psychological well-being in order to find salvation or healing. It is an ongoing process to heal after exploitation and trauma. You are simply their ride out. To believe that you are anything greater than this is hubris.

What You Will Need:
    *A team of support, including especially a Survivor-leader. This book is a start but it is *not* a substitute for guidance from an experienced survivor. If you are not a survivor yourself, do not attempt

extractions until you befriend someone who is, and be sure they are fully committed to your home team, to help you during the extraction and to give additional support to the victim. (If nothing else, you may not fully appreciate either the emotions and trauma the extractee is going through in the event, or even the language she or he may use to communicate about these. The survivor will.) When we do an extraction we have Laurin, our survivor leader, either in the car doing the actual contact and extraction, or at home on the phone almost hourly.

*A home-base team. In addition to the survivor-leader, have three or so people at home or in the city of extraction (or both) who know your plan, your routes, and your time frame; and who can provide any additional resources you might need. This support could include emergency funds for medical needs you might not have known about, extra clothing or shoes, and to be sure of communication redundancies—if more than one person knows you've been held up in traffic they can inform others when your arrival is delayed, etc. and corroborate the information.

*Knowledge of and patience for the victim's situation. Statistically, leaving is the most dangerous time of a victim's life. As with any abusive relationship termination, it takes *many* efforts and incredible self-will to leave an enmeshed abusive relationship. The average success comes at between seven and twelve attempts. Be aware of this, and be aware of the enormous courage it is taking for the victim to become a survivor.

*Laid-out plans, with approximate times, and alternate routes to and from the city of extraction.

*A car in working order.

*A full tank of gas.

*An extraction partner (two people is optimum, one to contact and one to drive; more could be crowded, one is not enough).

*Charged cell phones and back-up chargers for both partners.

*Enough money for gas, lodging, and food for the trip.

*Motrin, aspirin, or Tylenol.

*Tunes for the trip in, but not necessarily out— your survivor may need quiet.

*Supplies for the car trip: the backseat should ideally be for the survivor alone. In the back seat, have a fresh and clean pillow and blanket, a bottle or travel mug with water and maybe another drink of their preference.

*A destination, for short-term "landing spot" until a suitable program can be found for the survivor. We bring survivors directly to our RSM-run safe house. This is not a full recovery program or rehabilitation center (we are not equipped for such), but a safe quiet place to sleep, breathe, and re-adjust for a while. If at all possible, arrange with your team to have at least a room in a home (secure, comfortable, quiet) available for the survivor's first days out of the life. Do not use *any* shelter that your survivor-leader has not checked out, and vetted the staff etc. As noted, most homeless shelters will refuse victims of trafficking because most victims have a "record" of "crime." The "place to land" should not in any way "re-victimize" the survivor.

The Order of Operations

For RSM, rides out have followed this order:

      *Outreach. Through giveaways, sometimes our own outreach events, but also at parades and events like Pride Day, we provide seasonally appropriate goodie-bags with snacks, condoms, lip-gloss or hand cream, gloves or scarves, and always, our card, which has the hotline number. As enough cards reach the right hands, we get calls from people wanting a ride out.

      *Calls, planning. After a victim calls us consistently and we have built up trust on both sides of the equation, we begin planning the extraction with her or him depending on how to most safely make contact and give the ride.

      *Notification of the teams/board. RSM Board of Directors are all alerted to the trip, and the plans are shared so everyone knows what is planned and what should be happening in real time.

      *Trip preparations, including taking (never making) any possible final calls from the victim. Gassing the car, buying bottle water, etc.

      *Trip and extraction

      *Intake into safe house and placement of survivor in suitable program

Part 2: The Story of an Extraction.

The following "example" is a composite
narrative of what an extraction might look like. We
have extracted many people; none of the following is
any one person's "real" story. We have used details
from many experiences to make this composite to show
how we have gone about this in the past. All identifying
details are obscured or changed so that we can ensure
anonymity of our survivor clientele. We'll tell it in the
first person from Laurin's point of view, but again, it's
not a historical "case," just fictionalized story of how an
extraction could work.

Tuesday night, 4.am. The phone rings, my heart
beats fast; I was just barely falling asleep.

I clear my throat, touch the answer button.
"RockStarr Ministries, can I help you?"

There's a pause, and then a quiet breath,
"Hello? Is this, is this the place that helps—?" She
stops and then says, "I'm calling this number from a
card I got in a bag? Bag with condoms and candy and
lotions—is this RockStarrs?"

"Yes, it is. Can we help you? Are you safe?"

There's a gasp, and the voice begins to tremble.
"I'm, I'm okay for right now, but my I don't want
boyfriend to find out. I think I'm pregnant but I don't
want to ask for a test—" She stops and gets her voice
steady, continues, "He was . . . well, we had a fight, and
I remembered your card. I thought about when I saw
you giving out bags. Do you think, maybe, I could leave

him? I mean, he's usually great, used to be so—and I still love him but I—I not really sure he loves me. He's different, he's getting mean, he hits me more now I if I don't—" She stops and I can hear her breathing change as she begins to cry.

I wait for a few moments. "Honey? Are you okay now? What's your name? Are you safe right now?"

She begins to say something more but there is noise in the background and she hangs up abruptly. It is probably her "boyfriend," and it's better for her that she didn't answer me.

I check the phone timer. The call only lasted about two minutes. But it is the two minutes that could change her life, if she will follow through. I pray she will. This girl is thinking about leaving, but I know she's not ready for that break now. I hope she will call back, and I save her number—but I don't have her name. Instead I put in "Victim," then change it to SURVIVOR, and the date. I pray again for her, and ask God to keep her safe and give her the courage to get out. It will have to be her initiative; I will not pursue; we never, never call back; pimps check phone logs; pimps sometimes answer their girls' phones.

I close my eyes knowing I won't sleep. I remember being there. Remember when I had a "boyfriend" just like that. A "lover" who groomed me gradually, "loving" me and giving me everything, telling how beautiful I was, how great I was, how he wanted a life with me, a family, even. Before I knew what he was, or what I was, before I knew such words as "human trafficking" could be used to describe what he was doing.

His voice echoes in my head from years ago: "I do so much for you baby. What you going to do for me now?"

And I said no to his "exchange"—what he wanted me to "do for him" was to go with another man. And that was the night he beat me so hard I could not walk for two days.

I said no the second time too.

It never takes more than twice.

I don't sleep for three more hours. As the sky outside turns a purpley grey, I drift off into dreamless sleep, one more prayer for this girl in my heart.

This is not enough to go on. But it is a start, for her. For one little soul, making that call was actually something bigger than the whole world.

She does call again. Gradually I get more information, and she gets stronger, braver. In a few days, we have her name, and she has her conviction. This time the call comes at midnight. "Laurin, it's Lila again. I'm ready. I'm ready. He beat down one of my friends, and I know he's only gonna get worse with me, I know it. I didn't tell him about being pregnant. Don't want to start showing. Can you come get me?"

"You sound better. Where are you?"

We talk for a half an hour this time. I make her promise me over and over that she's ready and won't back out. "Because if you are really sure you want to leave, let me tell you, you are going to have to do the hardest part of leaving by yourself. Are you ready to hard things?"

She says yes, she is.

"Well that's good then! I will talk to my board of directors about securing you a place in the safe house, and give you the final plan next time we talk."

I give her some text numbers for email options—she has access to the internet twice a day when her "boyfriend" has her post pictures and ads on BackPage and some other websites that advertise human flesh.

When she calls back, she confirms again that she is serious about leaving.

After making a firm plan, within a day or so we will meet her in her city.

Lila's pimp has tight control over her and the other women he prostitutes. We have to be careful. It isn't possible to meet her anywhere but the hotel she "works" from.

Her job is to go to the front desk to refresh the room's towels. Chris, our driver's job is to have the car idling in a close parking place on the back side of the lobby, while I go into the hotel. My job is to meet Lila. I tell the hotel clerk I'm meeting a friend to take her to the hospital for an emergency; is it ok for me to wait here for her?

I arrive ten minutes early and position myself in the lobby, to be hypervigilant and aware of all the exits. As if on cue, she walks through the door at exactly

11:00. She is wearing a strap tee shirt and shorts. She carries nothing. She is not even wearing shoes.

Our eyes meet and I call her by name, "Lila."

She nods and walks toward me.

I'm taller than Lila, and when I put my arms around her she is shaking a bit.

"It's time to go, Baby," I say, loud enough for the clerk to know I'm done here.

She swallows and meets my eye for a fraction of a second. I turn and put my arm through hers, and we leave through the back exit where the car is idling and Chris is watching, ready to drive.

"Back seat, stay low," I say.

I get in front, and Chris pulls the car out of the parking lot.

It is quiet until we are a half a block away. Then Lila's voice from low in the backseat whispers, "This is the farthest away I been for four days."

I take a breath. "Ok, Lila, we talked about this before, and it's on the intake agreement. I'm going to need your cell phone. It's too easy for people to find you with it. You need to let me have it now."

"No, it's ok, I'll give it to you when we get there. I got it on airplane—"

"Lila." I turn in the passenger seat and hold out my hand. She looks at me and her eyes flash with defiance. Then fear. "He's following us," she says.

I'm not distracted. "See then?" I say. "Reason to give me the phone. This is part of the deal, Lila, and we talked about it. I know having it makes you feel in control, but it's how he can track you, and it's how you can slip back *out* of control. Give me your phone, or we cannot do this."

She looks at the device in its glittery case, her hand wrapped tight around it. "What are you going to do with it? When do I get it back?"

"At this point, it doesn't matter, Boo. But I'll tell you. I'm going to take the battery out and store it in a different place than the phone. I don't want him find you, and I don't want him to find my safe house and all the people who need the safe house to be *safe*. Do you?"

Lila looks at me with a diminishing shade of resentment, and then she looks out the back window of the car. She hands me her phone.

"Thank you," I say, and I pull the battery. In my head, I picture myself glaring at her pimp and saying something very very rude to him, but I say none of this out loud!

Chris speaks easily, gently, no tension in his voice, though the tension in the car is thick, mingled angry and terrified. "Ok, Lila, I'm not sure anyone's following, but I'm going to lose him if we are. I'm not going to go fast or weave around because I don't want to get pulled over. I'll talk you through what I'm doing as I do it, Ok? This next intersection I'm going to turn right, and watch to see if anybody behind me also turns right. I'll do that four times: here—" He slows to a full stop, his signal on, and takes the turn at normal speed.

"And then at this next block," he says.

I can hear Lila drinking the entire contents of the water bottle we had for her in the back seat.

Chris takes the next corner. It doesn't appear to me that anyone is following us, but Chris turns twice more and puts us back on course to leave the city.

The trip home is mostly silent. We listen to music (hip hop, R and B). She sleeps through most of the long highway straights and small towns and cities we pass through. Probably the most sleep she has had in days too. We take our first rest stop out of state to fill the car and eat a little, and we buy some sandals for Lila's bare feet.

At early light we pull into the driveway of the safe house.

"Lila? Wake up, honey, wake up Lila. We're here."

Because of her trafficker fears, we have put her in a largest basement room, hidden away from the street, with strong door and locks, and her own television set. There are fresh linens, and a basket of donated toiletries on her bed. She seems pleased with this arrangement, and I tell her we'll talk in the morning. When she wakes up, we finish the intake form we had begun during our last week's conversations. We get her an appointment with our doctor, and because she is pregnant we take extra cautions to ensure the safety of her and the pregnancy.

Part 3: Preparing plans for Extraction

The best extractions happen with the best-laid plans. Though planning always depends on the individual situation, there are some touchpoints that can be prepared for, including the intake, the distraction, the meet-up, and the drive.

The Intake:

Before setting things into motion, you should have the most information possible about the situation you are getting into. This is the phone call stage. It's important to establish a rapport with your client. It's important to stay emotionally stable, sympathetic, kind and strong. Never express doubt or fear about any possible problems; your victim will provide those! It is your job to have a concise and clear plan of action and not to doubt it. Talk on the phone with the victim often. Do not call her (or him). Do not jump in or move to extract after a single call. You need time (and your client needs time) to build trust and good faith on both ends of the relationship.

As you talk, write down the information necessary for filling out your intake form. These are available for a nominal fee from several organizations; but be sure yours is clear about your expectations for your clientele, and set some rock-solid rules for the ride out and the first days out.

For us these include:

1. No cell phones
2. No internet or devices that access the internet (including walks to the local library)
3. No contact with persons from your former life
4. No drug usage beyond what our doctor prescribes
5. Willingness to submit to random drug testing
6. No fighting, violence or threatening language
7. Mandatory attendance and attention at debriefings from our survivor-leaders
8. No destruction of property
9. Willing participation in household chores

Unwillingness to abide by any of these will result in immediate dismissal from the program.

The next step to plan for is the way things will happen. Ask about what a typical day looks like for your client, so you can plan on an unnoticable place and time to meet. If she (he) has freedom to move around or is "working" out of a hotel or motel. If a client is mobile, it broadens your options; you could meet outside a police station, a library, a fast food place or convenience store, etc., anywhere the pimp is unlikely to be watching. It is better that a client not wait outside an establishment, or risk being seen by her pimp or harassed for loitering. If she gets to your designated spot early (say at a Denny's or other chain restaurant), then it's good for her to go to the back of the shop and order a coffee (which we will pay for when we arrive). Usually if we meet in a relatively public space like this, it is simply a matter of walking out together and getting in the car.

If she is in a hotel or motel, she will probably need a distraction.

The Distraction

Depending on how closely the client is being watched, she will need to leave her hotel room for enough time that she can be safely escorted out before raising suspicions back in the room. She cannot pack a bag or bring anything with her—even a purse is a signal that she is not coming back.

Make sure you are in place at the designated meet-up during the distraction because these tactics will only work once.

When the meet-up time comes, the client has to create a good reason to "briefly" leave the room. Ideas for distractions:

Spill something messy. Breaking a bottle of liquid foundation makeup on the floor will require a broom and towels and cleaners to set right. The errand to fetch a broom and towels will take longer than an ice-bucket run. Fingernail polish on clothes is also a big mess and needs special attention and probably stuff not found in the room.

Flush a pair of panties down the toilet. Hotel rooms usually do not have plungers; she will have to go to the front desk to report the problem; you can be waiting for her there. Be sure she turns off the water supply under the toilet and does not leave it running; further damage to the hotel room could bring the pimp or john to the front desk too.

The Meet-up

Be cheerful and nonchalant; greet each other by name and then don't waste time talking, just make sure you get to the car as quickly and unobtrusively as possible. It's good to have a small throw blanket or hoodie to toss over her head and shoulders as she leaves. Open the back door for her, lock and close it and have her lie down across the seats. Get in your seat and buckle your belt. The car should have a full tank and have immediate access to an easy exit; you should not have to circle the parking lot or execute three-point turns to leave.

The Drive

Plan to follow all traffic laws religiously. Know the shortest route from the meet-up to the nearest highway onramp, and then just drive. Try to get several hours behind you before needing to have a pit stop; state lines are good.

Plan to move clients a good distance from the city of their trafficking and their pimp control. Never keep clients in the same city where they were trafficked. Geographical distance is their friend—the further away from their trafficking city the better.

Final notes on planning:

From her final commitment to leave, do not wait more than 24 hours to get her out. Final plans should made in the last phone call; everyone involved should know the plan, including estimated times of arrival and departure.

Make sure each person is clear about his or her roles and functions.

Be calm and professional; it's important to keep the situation under control. This is a scary time for the client, but no one should give in to the feelings of panic or fear. Since you will not always know how hard it might be for any given client, it's vital for you and your partner to remain free from drama or nervousness.

Part 4: Trish's Story

Trish had called in early November and told us her situation. She had found RSM information from her pimp. He had told her (untruthfully) that he had owned Laurin and that she had a "Home for Retired Hos," and then taunted her, "If you tired of it here why don't you go to her?"

She did. She told us she was in jeopardy of losing her children, and the judge had told her that getting away from (as she put it) her "boyfriend" was her last chance to retain her parental rights. At the time she told us the name of her social worker, who was thrilled at the chance to get Trish out. We were waiting for her to call from Vegas to arrange her ride.

The next time she called was two months later. She'd been beaten by a trick and was beyond desperate to leave. But she was in Los Angeles, now, instead of Vegas. She was in one of the most heavily-infested gang areas of the city. This meant the drive for us would be longer.

She did not have a phone, and called us from her mother's landline. Her mother had no problem with Trish, but she had a dozen more kids in a one bedroom apartment, and also had a history of being trafficked herself. Also fortunately for us, Trish's mother was on speaking terms with the pimp who was controlling Trish, and she usually saw Trish every day. She didn't pose a threat to the pimp, and so we asked her if she'd be willing to help with Trish's extraction, and she agreed.

This trafficker was known to be erratic and a frequent drug user. He didn't allow Trish any form of communication. The last time we spoke to her she assured us that she was ready to leave at any time, since we might not be able to talk again before the extraction.

When we got to LA, we contacted her mom, who was willing to come with us to meet with Trish. Because of her inability to talk on the phone, this was our only "in" to finding her. Trish happened to be a few blocks down on the same street on which her mom lived. It was a two-way street, with heavy traffic, police at both ends, circling helicopters. After our second drive-by we were able to locate Trish's mother and I (Laurin) stepped out of the car long enough to shake her hand and get her into the back seat. As she directed us, we went to the motel where Trish was working.

Our driver then pulled over to an illegal parking spot and laid low in the idling car.

I spoke briefly with mom as if I was a social worker, and she walked me through the labyrinth of crack fiends and tweakers to Trish's room. I stood back several feet as her mom knocked, and when Trish answered the door she had a trick in her room. Her mother introduced me as a social worker who needed to talk with her about her kids, and I needed a moment alone with Trish.

She was packed and she said she hadn't seen her pimp in several days. She told the trick to wait, that she would be right back, and we made our way as unobtrusively as possible back to the parked car. She got in the back seat and we quickly pulled away from the motel. Now we had the task of her mother being dropped off in the same neighborhood without Trish being seen. So with her face hidden and staying low in the seat, she said tearful goodbyes to her family through her mom.

We assured her mother that we would be taking her straight out, and that with the traffic as heavy as it was, we could only pause briefly for her to exit the car. We dropped her quickly about two blocks from her home and got on our pre-planned route out of the city onto the freeway. Even though Trish told us that she had eaten, and that she was not sleep deprived, she fell asleep almost instantly and did not wake up for the entire twelve hour drive home.

Part 5: After the Ride Out

In general, after we give someone a ride out, we've all been in the car for an extended period of time, which can be exhausting. We bring them to the safe house where the room has been prepared with clean sheets and towels, and we have some donated clothing in a variety of sizes that we keep on hand for those who have nothing.

In our case basement rooms are usually preferred because they feel safer and more private away from street noises, but be sensitive to individual needs. Survivors may feel more comfortable nearer to the director, or with daylight from windows, etc. Our safe house has enough variety of rooms that they can choose according to their needs. Be sensitive and aware.

We put soaps, chapsticks, feminine supplies, lotions, and other goodies in a basket as a welcome gift. We usually can offer a meal, but find it's most common that on arrival, everybody is ready for a nap!

It's necessary to have a good stock of food in lots of varieties, being aware of dietary needs such as allergies. Clients are free to help themselves to the kitchen, to be able to cook for themselves. If they want to bake a cake at three a.m., have cake mixes around.

Have plenty of milk, soda, kool-aids, canned soups, top ramen noodles, breads, frozen meats, fresh fruits and vegetables, all of which might have been very scarce in their street life. Many prostituted people live almost exclusively on McDonalds and other fast food, so something hot and home-cooked can be a God-send.

Because our house is an emergency stop-off, and not a program for full recovery, we do not have a regiment of time schedules or programming activities. There are no locked doors, though curfew is at nine thirty. We allow survivors to be alone, with some frequent checks on their well-being, but just a tap on the door and a question. Let them know where the laundry, food stores, kitchen, bathroom supplies are, and allow them to have their own sovereignty for the first time possibly in years.

Sometime in the first day of their extraction, we will finish the intake forms. We make it clear that this is not a forced situation; they are able to leave at any time. Most stay because it is safe, their pimps cannot find them, and they have a new identity to think about.

We have had a flexible schedule in terms of length of stay also. As few as three days or as long as two months, but again it depends on the situation. If you are indeed a ride out, and not a Safe House (as we have done both in the past); have a network of destinations for their fit, and begin to ask the questions about life away from trafficking: Do they need a GED? Do they need medical attention, dental help, physical therapy? Do they need specific types of counseling programs or drug treatment? Do they want religious ministry? When those needs are addressed, the survivor can prepare for further habilitation.

We have had most luck with one client survivor (and their children, if necessary) staying at the safe house at a time. . Even the best roommates can be a source of stress for those recently out from under external control. It is quieter and easier for our survivor house guests to rest with few distractions and no fuss about the resources, such as food and bathrooms; and privacy itself is likely something the survivor has not had the luxury of enjoying very much in her or his previous life.

It's necessary that the landing spot be staffed with knowledgeable survivor(s) and/or fully trained companions. Clientele should not outnumber staff. We also have a computer but with limited wifi (we do not want traffickers finding survivors), a television set and dvd player and lots of movies and shows, and of course shelves of books to read, and a well-stocked kitchen for cooking. Each survivor contributes to the housework and yard work.

Each is invited, but never required, to attend worship services and/or auxiliary meetings with church groups of their choice.

Conclusion: Life after The Life

We cannot reveal identifying information about the persons who have caught their rides out with us. But we can report that we have received grateful messages from survivors who have gone on to recovery programs, some who have healed from physical injuries and hurts, some who have applied for and gone on to employment, schools, and professional jobs training programs. As mentioned earlier, there have sadly been some of "our" survivors (fewer than fingers on one hand) who have possibly slipped back into relationships that are destructive or abusive. We remember—and we hope they do as well—that it takes many efforts to leave a deeply-imprinted pattern of life, and many efforts to leave a trafficker. We are still here for them. They only need to call us.

Happily, the vast majority of our riders have stayed safe and have found a way back to self-acceptance and self-care after their nightmare of trafficked life. One soul at a time, we hope to make a difference for those caught in human trafficking. We hope this booklet is helpful to the anti-trafficking community, and wish all efforts Godspeed, in offering and providing the needed Ride Out.